I Am Who You Seek

Inspired Writings
By
Sandra J Yearman

Seraphim Publishing LLC

WE WILL BRING LIGHT TO ALL THE DARK PLACES

Registered trademark-Sandra J Yearman
Seraphim Publishing
438 Water St
Cambridge, WI 53523

Copyright © 2008 Sandra J Yearman
Produced in the United States of America
Author : Sandra J Yearman
Editor: Sandra J Yearman
Cover Design by Sandra J Yearman
Layout and design by Sandra J Yearman

All rights reserved. No part of this book may be reproduced, stored in or introduced into a retrieval system, or transmitted, in any form or by any means, electronic or mechanical, including photocopying or recording or otherwise copied for public or private use—other than for "fair use" as brief quotations embodied in articles and reviews—without written permission from the author.

Library of Congress Control Number: 2009900817
ISBN: 978-0-9815791-2-2
First Edition

God's Voice Filled Creation
As He Sent His Holy Lamb
I AM The God Of Your Fathers
I AM WHO I AM
Amen
Amen
Amen

CONTENTS

DEDICATION

I Am Who You Seek...................7
The Great I AM........................9
Holy One.................................11
4th of July..............................13
Eternity...................................15
Jesus..17
God Of Old.............................19
First Light...............................21
Heaven Knows........................23

SEEKING LIGHT IN THE DARKNESS

When The Death Masks Crumble............26
Pass The Holy Tests...................27
Each Creation Is Unique............30
The Insanity Is Within Us..........33
Esther......................................35
What Is Man's Destiny..............37
Dressings.................................39

CONTENTS

The Horsemen Ride.................................41
Man-Forged Sword..................................44
God Has the Answers.............................46
What Illusion Are We In.........................48
Without Their Wings..............................50
Grace From Above..................................52
Path..54
To Bring The Heavens Near...................55
Miracles..57
The Prophet..60
A Tiny Light...62

COMING HOME

God's Gifts...66
Jesus Loves...68
Believe..70
The Angels Dance In Heaven................71
Angel Dreams..73
And We Dance......................................75
Confirmation...77

Dedication

I Am Who You Seek

As I lay dying
My spirit burdened and meek
I called out to my Lord
His Holy Face to seek

And in my dying hour
A Voice I heard speak
'My child, My child'
'I AM who you seek'

I felt my body quiver
I felt my body shake
My tears were flowing
I was cleansed of my hate

When my legs would hold me
I stood up from my bed
My body filled with strength
I no longer walked among the dead

I turned my face to Heaven
And through tears, I cried
Forgive me Lord
I will always walk at Your side

My life was changed forever
The moment I heard God's Voice speak
I soar among the living
God's Face I will always seek

Amen Amen Amen

The Great I Am

God's Voice filled creation
As He sent His Holy Lamb
I AM the God of your fathers
I AM WHO I AM

You will know Me
You will understand
You will remember the Love of Heaven
You will leave this world of man

God's Voice filled creation
As He sent His Holy Lamb
I AM the God of your fathers
I AM WHO I AM

Blessed are My children
Whose faith withstands all
The trials and temptations
The large and the small

God's Voice filled creation
As He sent His Holy Lamb
I AM the God of your fathers
I AM WHO I AM

And you will know My Blessings
For Love transcends all
Faith can move mountains
Faith answers the Call

God's Voice filled creation
As He sent His Holy Lamb
I AM the God of your fathers
I AM WHO I AM

Amen Amen Amen

Holy One

Holy Spirit
One in Three
Inspiration, Fire
The Comforter sent from Thee

Performs miracles
Saves the souls
Moves the mountains
Heaven's goals

Fills the heart
With Song and Praise
Blesses creation
All their days

Through the darkness
Light He brings
Heavenly Father
Angels sing

Holy Spirit
Three in One
Heavenly Father
Holy Son

Amen Amen Amen

4th Of July

One nation under God
One nation
As He died to make men Holy, let us die to make men free
One nation
His Truth is marching on…

One nation surrendered to God at the birth of its government
One nation where the laws understand the uniqueness and beauty of all God's creations
One nation where God
can be worshipped
Where God can be worshipped
Where God can be worshipped

One nation that is trying to be so
politically correct
That we are allowing darkness to
dictate where we worship
How we worship
When and where we can utter
God's Name

One nation under God
When did we lose our souls...

Amen Amen Amen

Eternity

Lights in the sky
Holy flames from Heaven
Angels and friends
Sins are forgiven

Love beyond boundaries
Life beyond fear
Welcomes creation
Wipes away tears

Love of the Ages
Family of Old
Glory to God
On Wings of Gold

Lights so brilliant
To cleanse all hearts
Love transcends
We will never be apart

Amen Amen Amen

Jesus

Jesus was tempted by darkness
On the trail of tears
In His Holiness
He conquered a world of fears

Demons have nothing to offer
Demons have nothing to give
Jesus conquered satan
Jesus taught man how to live

How can you tempt One who is Holy
When He already possess all
Jesus showed that satan had to no power
Satan has nothing at all

God has everything to offer
God has everything to give
He created us to be His children
He died so we may live

Amen Amen Amen

God Of Old

The God of our fathers
The God of the twelve tribes
The God of Jerusalem
Saved all our lives

He gave us the commandments
He gave us the laws
He gave us Salvation
He gave us All

But man is never happy
With the gifts that he has
He destroys and he changes
He is rarely glad

And private agendas
Cloud interpretations
And all of creation
Suffers determinations

Go back to the Father
The God of old
Follow His Word
As He had it told

Amen Amen Amen

First Light

Light of the Heavens
Light of the skies
Man through eternity
Prays and asks why

Dawn of the darkness
Dawn of the soul
Dawn of creation
Song that was told

Sung by the Angels
Sung by some men
Song of creation
Throughout all ends

Son of the Father
Spirit and Three
Song of creation
Salvation and Thee

Amen Amen Amen

Heaven Knows

Only Heaven knows our fears and motivations
Our crimes and our deeds
Our prayers and tribulations
Our wants and our needs

Our deepest desires
The dreams that we long
Our passions and fires
The words to our songs

Nothing is hidden
Nothing is obscure
Nothing exists in the shadows
No voice is too weak to hear

Heaven knows our frailties
Heaven knows our strengths
Heaven knows our actions
Heaven knows the length

That we will go to accomplish
When we will end the race
If we conquer our darkness
And seek His Holy Face

Amen Amen Amen

Seeking Light In The Darkness

When The Death Masks Crumble

When the death masks crumble
Glory will be our Home
Jesus will come for us
No more in darkness to roam

When the death masks crumble
The tests have been complete
The trials and tribulations
Of life on earth we meet

When the death masks crumble
And death has lost its sting
Jesus will come for us
The music of Heaven will ring

Amen Amen Amen

Pass The Holy Tests

In their fear and ignorance
They refused to take His Hand
The children of God
Wanted a man-king to rule the land

They could not see the purpose
They did not understand the gifts
Their fears had over taken
Their faith had gone a drift

They sought the obsessions of the body
They sought the world they could see
Limited by their frailties
Inconceivable were their needs

God sent them what they asked for
They chose a king of clay
Large and intimidating
They thought he would protect them
all their days

But Saul had all the frailties
And needs of humanity
Darkness over took him
The children of God soon could see

He was not the answer
He did not past the tests
God sent another
Who did his very best

God in His wisdom
Would not let His children down
He sent them a Holy King
Wearing a Holy Crown

The child warrior
On bended knees did pray
Surrendered to His Lord
Faith was his armor, glory were his days

This child king united the known worlds
And taught them of the Lord
He was blessed by God
He balanced the Scales and Sword

Amen Amen Amen

Each Creation Is Unique

Mountains that reach forever
Blue crystal were our seas
Flora that flourished
Fauna that met our needs

What have we done to nature
The gifts God blessed us with
Why do we destroy what sustains us
What is the unholy bid

Beauty beyond comprehension
Destroyed for profit and greed
Why do we destroy what sustains us
What is the unholy need

Is it an unconscious way of
committing suicide
Or souls that we have sold
That we would destroy all that sustains
The Holy gifts of old

The victims are the innocents
That fall prey to profit and greed
Why do we destroy what sustains us
What are our unholy needs

God save us from our darkness
Save the victims here
Show us the Light of Heaven
Make Your Presence clear

Forgive us for our actions
Forgive us for our greed
Forgive us for calling to darkness
To fulfill our unholy needs

Remind us we are Your children
Each creation is unique
Your Love beyond comprehension
Your Holy Chalice to drink

Amen Amen Amen

The Insanity Is Within Us

The dark face of humanity
The death masks that we wear
Makes us unique among creation
For the oaths we choose to swear

We say that we are empowered
With more blessings from above
Yet we use the Holy Sword
To kill each other and the dove

We believe we are superior
To the rest of God's creations
Yet we fail to pass the tests
As seen by our mutilations

Do we believe we are more powerful
Because we kill the rest
If God gave us this garden
Have we passed the Holy test

God forgive us for our ignorance
And the blindness of our ways
Help us to understand Your Holiness
Break through this darkened haze

Help us to understand
The lessons You showed us from old
The power is with the Spirit
Not the clay, not the gold

To kill all that we are blessed with
Is not a sign of strength
The insanity is within us
We go to any length

To obtain money and power
To feed our unholy greed
God save us from ourselves
Bless us with what we really need

Amen Amen Amen

Esther

Strong was her faith in God
Her honor and her grace
She asked God to use her
She helped to save a human race

Because of her great beauty
She was called before a king
To grace him with her presence
She brought the Spirit in

Gentle was her temperament
Yet dedicated to the Lord
She helped to save God's children
From the butchers sword

How God works His miracles
Is often beyond the human eye
He can take a dove
And teach a world to fly

Faith can move mountains
It moves the coldest hearts
The Spirit of the Lord
From His children will not part

Esther became a queen of men
Yet an Angel she could be
She followed the Voice of the Lord
When others would flee

Wonder at your purpose
Is there a reason we are here
Is it to wallow in the darkness
Or miracles to bear

Amen Amen Amen

What Is Man's Destiny

There are sounds of war in
the distance
God save this family here
Clouds of smoke announce
hell's presence
The heat of flames to sear

Is destruction man's destiny
Is death man's fate
Does man not see through the hatred
and fear
Has man already entered hell's gate

What prompts us to destruction
Why do we give our demons full
command
Do we hate ourselves so much
That we want to destroy this world of
man

Lord a voice is crying from the darkness
I fear the other voices are already dead
Cleanse us from our darkness
And this hate filled course we led

God help us to conquer our demons
Help us to change our fates
Help us to call to Heaven
Save creation before it is too late

Amen Amen Amen

Dressings

Dressings on the windows
Dressings on the stand
Dressings created by all of us
Are illusions in the world of man

Images in the media
Pictures we create
Illusions of the masses
Perpetuate fear and hate

When we speak of reality
What do we really mean
Since the guise of man
Changes what is seen

Ask God to help us see through the illusions
The images that are false
The smoke screens and diversions
That cover what is lost

Let the death masks be shattered
And the faces exposed
Let the Truths be revealed
As only Heaven knows

Amen Amen Amen

The Horsemen Ride

The horsemen rode among us
In a fiery rage
To spread unholy darkness
To set the unholy stage

All the sins of hell
Were manifest in their beings
Their plague conquered the earth
And infected all human beings

The horsemen rode with thunder
The horsemen rode with zeal
To destroy all creation
And pervert God's Holy will

And the children among them
Asked the horsemen in
To dwell with them
To teach them of sin

The horsemen ride through the
centuries
Their paths are clear
For the children of creation
Always call them near

The children became the horsemen
And carried their names
They infected others with the plague
And spread sins of the same

Time blows upon the winds
Centuries march on
The children of creation
Forgot about the Holy Son

When will we stop calling to
the horsemen
When will we understand our place
When will we all return to God
And ask to be filled with Holy Grace

Amen Amen Amen

Man-Forged Sword

Moses was an anchor
Moses was blessed
Moses saved God's children
Moses passed the Holy tests

Moses faced the darkness
With the shield of faith
He preformed miracles
Through God's Loving Grace

Anyone can become mighty
If they surrender to the Lord
There is more power in faith
Than in any man-forged sword

Darkness has no foothold
When you call the Savior near
Light will always dissolve the darkness
God will always hear

Bring God into your life
Ask Him to stand before
When He answers your prayers
Open all your doors

Prepare a table for Him
Ask Him to become part of your life
Ask Him to help you conquer
The darkness and the strife

Anyone can become mighty
If they surrender to the Lord
There is more power in faith
Than in any man-forged sword

Amen Amen Amen

God Has The Answers

Images are pervasive
The children are dying here
Every where you look
Everything you hear

Yet hope is on the horizon
For those who believe in the Son
God over came death
A battle already won

Yet we each have our own cross to carry
Our own path that we must find
Do we have a purpose here
This question has been asked throughout all times

Pray and He will answer
Ask Him the questions in your mind
Only the Source can give the answers
The secrets you will find

Amen Amen Amen

What Illusion Are We In

This world is made of illusions
As if we were on a movie screen
Story after story
We forget what movie we are in

What then is our purpose for being here
What are the Holy tests
Man has asked through the ages
Yet the answers seem to elude even the very best

Is it to conquer the body
With its darkness and its pain
And find the truth of Heaven
Our Holiness to gain

Is it possible the answers are before us
And perhaps have always been
The answer is to conquer the darkness
of this world
And return to where we begin

Amen Amen Amen

Without Their Wings

Will as strong as iron
Love beyond all bounds
Hair as black as night
Music were her sounds

A friend who stayed with me always
A friend who watches me from the sky
A friend who broke my heart
The day she had to die

Some memories never leave us
And hers will always stay
In my heart forever
Her actions and her ways

God sends us friends as anchors
God sends us friends as wings
God blesses us with their presence
Even though some are unseen

Thank You God for all the messengers
And friends who have blessed my life
Who have come with perfect timing
To help me in my strife

Thank You for the blessings
And love they do bring
Angels must walk this earth
Some without their wings

Amen Amen Amen

Grace From Above

There was a man of darkness
Who claimed to be the heir to God's throne
Like so many others
In his thoughts and ways he was not alone

God in His Holy Wisdom
Made an example of this man
With the Grace of Heaven
Transformation began

This man who had persecuted the children of God
Was saved by God's Grace and Love
God changed Paul's life
Paul praised the Lord above

The amazing Grace of Heaven
Can change even the darkest heart
The Father Loves His children
From us He will never be apart

Amen Amen Amen

Path

There is no man so mighty
That he cannot be destroyed by his
choices in life
History has shown us greatly
Alone we can not withstand this life of
strife

Ask the Lord to carry
Ask the Lord to bring
The Holy Spirit into your life
The Heavenly Songs to sing

For we are not here all alone
Perhaps to past the tests
We have to find the path to God
In the maze of all the rest

Amen Amen Amen

To Bring The Heavens Near

Who would not remember
The wonder of His birth
Who would choose a life of clay
Who upon this earth

Yet we make these decisions always
Each and every day
We are tested constantly
Choose Spirit or choose clay

Are there no more mystics
Or poets who question "why"
Are we immobilized by technology
Do we wonder what is beyond the
skies

When is man satisfied
With what is before his eyes
Do we call out to God
And ask Him "why"

Ask Him how to transcend the boundaries
How to break the darkest hold
How to bring Light to this world
How to change humanity's mold

Do we call out to the Heavens
And ask if they can hear
And ask if they will speak with us
To bring the Heavens near

Amen Amen Amen

Miracles

People have ideas
Of where the power lies
God has always shown us
That Miracles can come in any guise

Jesus fed the thousands
With but a few fish and bread
He sent His disciples into all the worlds
To teach what Jesus said

These humble servants of the Lord
Were faithful followers of the Son
God gave them what they needed
They spoke in many tongues

People have ideas
Of where the power lies
God has always shown us
That Miracles can come in any guise

David conquered Goliath
As armies of men were filled with fear
His faith carried him
God kept him near

Moses saved a nation
Esther saved a race
Elijah called down fire
All these servants were filled with
God's Grace

People have ideas
Of where the power lies
God has always shown us
That Miracles can come in any guise

Yet the most incredible Miracle
Of them all
Was a baby born
In a humble stall

Amen Amen Amen

The Prophet

Elijah was a prophet
He was a Holy man
Faithful to his God
He took a Holy stand

Elijah challenged the priests of darkness
Elijah challenged the king
Elijah spoke in God's Name
Elijah brought the Spirit in

God preformed miracles through him
For Elijah had passed the Holy tests
God used him as a teacher
A model for the rest

And when his days were numbered
And when his mission was done
God honored him greatly
And brought him back to where he
had begun

Amen Amen Amen

A Tiny Light

When all earthly lights were dissolved
in the darkness
A tiny light did shine
It grew in brightness
It grew in design

For God answered the prayers of an
Angel
A baby in all right
Who prayed for God to walk on earth
And dissolve the darkest night

And God in His Holiness
With Wisdom and with Grace
Answers the prayers of all who believe
Regardless of time and place

'Lord, if You hear me'
'We need Your Presence here'
'For creation is spinning out of control'
'And darkness claims all with fear'

'Your children seem to have forgotten Your Name'
'They seem to fear to pray'
'But, how else can they talk with You'
'And bring a brighter day'

So the Angel prayed for all of them
In their ignorance and lack of faith
That God would touch them with His Presence
With His Love and with His Grace

The Angel carried many
And sheltered many more
God answered all her prayers
So the world of man could soar

Amen Amen Amen

Coming Home

God's Gifts

To all the blessed beauties
That God has put on earth
Who give of their love
Who satisfy our thirst

With honor and compassion
With hearts filled with Grace
God blesses us with Angels
Irrelevant of race

The choice belongs to each of us
To whom we open the door
Do we allow them to touch our lives
Do we rebuke and ask for more

God in His perfect Wisdom
Sends us what we need
The choice is how we use it
The choice is how we plant the seed

Amen Amen Amen

Jesus Loves

Jesus loved the creatures
That others threw away
The sick and injured
He loved them all their days

Jesus loved the children
Who were tortured in the night
He wiped away their tears
He took away their fright

Jesus exposed the darkness
Jesus took a stand
Jesus taught God's meaning
To the world of man

Jesus said the Father
Would give us Love and Grace
If we followed in His footsteps
And took our rightful place

The Father Loves His children
Each and everyone
He sent His beloved Son to save them
A battle Heaven won

Yet many do not listen
Many do not heed
To emulate Jesus
Is the Holy Creed

Amen Amen Amen

Believe

Faith endured through the ages
Faith kingdoms upheld
Faith has changed futures
Faith prophesies tell

Sometimes questioning is a ritual
Sometimes questioning helps past the tests
Sometimes the chains are broken
With Faith we always perform our best

Believing is our Salvation
Believing is the key
Believing when all else fails
Is the final test from Thee

Amen Amen Amen

The Angels Dance In Heaven

The Angels dance in Heaven
As the Song of God is sung
As creation calls to Heaven
To return to where they begun

As the ancient rites of passage
And the Holy tests are done
As creation calls to Heaven
To return to where they begun

The missions are most Holy
The chosen are most blessed
God in all His Wisdom
Has saved the forgotten and distressed

The Light God sent from Heaven
Clearly showed the path
The children chose their Father
Not hell's horrid and dark wrath

There is jubilation in Heaven
The children chose their Home
To return to the Father
No more in the dark worlds to roam

Amen Amen Amen

Angel Dreams

Do the Angels dream in slumber
Do they understand
Do they have the same illusions
As the world of man

Are the Angels tested
Are they sent on Holy missions from above
Do they walk among us
As their missions of true Love

Do they whisper to us
Do we hear what they say
Or discard their voices
As an anomaly of the day

Can we really see them
Or does our mind play tricks
To keep us in the darkness
To control us in the pit

Why would God send us Angels
But to guide us through the tests
To send us His messages
To let us know that we are blessed

Amen Amen Amen

And We Dance

God I have tried to follow Your
footsteps
All the days of this long life
Sometimes I have fallen
Or gone astray in my strife

But I have noticed
That whenever I do not know where
I am
I see Your footprints
Appearing before me in the sand

I run to try and keep up
Then You carry me
Sometimes my prints get lost in Yours
And the difference I can not see

I know that when our walk has ended
Because I chose to take a Holy change
We will rejoice in Heaven
And Lord, with Angels dance

Amen Amen Amen

Confirmation

I call upon the Heavens
The Father, Spirit and Son
I pray that You will hear me
I ask to receive the Holy One

Father I believe in You
Father bless my faith
I ask that You forgive me
And fill me with Holy Grace

I surrender all I am
I surrender all
You sent Your Son to save us
To save us from the fall

I call upon the Heavens
To cleanse us from our sins
To bring Your Light to this world
The Holy Spirit to bring in

I promise I will follow
Where others have failed
I beg to fill me with the Spirit
That Holiness may prevail

And all my days I will honor
As the tears travel on my cheeks
For the Holy moments of the Lord
For it is You that I seek

Amen Amen Amen

You Will Know Me
You Will Understand
You Will Remember
The Love Of Heaven
You Will Leave This World Of Man
Amen
Amen
Amen

www.ingramcontent.com/pod-product-compliance
Lightning Source LLC
Chambersburg PA
CBHW051712040426
42446CB00008B/845